American Revolution

A Philosophical and Practical Guide

Michael Calpino

**Copyright 2012
J&M Publishing**

michaelcalpino.com

Other Books by the Author

AND HASHTICHAROT SMILED
Conversations in Radical Liberty

GENESIS, ZEN AND QUANTUM PHYSICS
A New Look at the Theology and Science of Creation

AN INCEPTION OF PIRACY
(Historical Fiction)

LEAVE ME ALONE
A Patriot's Plan to Restore Pride and Prosperity to America

AUTHENTIC CHRISTIANITY

MEMOIRS OF A FORMER AMERICAN

ISRAEL, THE GOYIM AND THE ETERNAL DESTINY OF MAN

WHAT HAPPENED?
How Biblical Judaism Became Christianity

ART FOR THE REVOLUTION

POLITICAL WRITINGS 2000-2010

RELIGIOUS WRITINGS

Introduction

The exercise of our God-given natural rights should not, indeed it cannot, depend on the good will of the powerful or the erudition and courage of our fellow man. Just because the vast majority choose to live in meek, subservient, ignorance is no reason for you or I to suffer the indignity of slavery.

The following is written for those to whom liberty is most dear. To my fellow Americans, of whom there are so few left. Certainly there are hundreds of millions who call themselves "Americans" because of the accident of their birth but a true American is one who holds in the highest esteem the eternal principles of liberty, self government, natural rights, honor and charity and has the courage to adhere to these principles in the face of even the most energetic tyranny. Of these there are precious few. Perhaps, because you are reading this, you are one, or have the desire to become one.

"If ye love wealth greater than liberty, the tranquility of servitude greater than the animating contest for freedom, go home from us in peace. We

seek not your council or your arms. Crouch down and lick the hand that feeds you. May your chains set lightly upon you; and may posterity forget that ye were our countrymen." Samuel Adams

For those of you for whom the fire of liberty burns brightly within your soul even as everything around you conspires to extinguish it, this is for you. I have felt your frustration. Every moment of every day we see politicians and bureaucrats passing laws and regulations that cinch the straightjacket of tyranny over our lives ever tighter and we are finding it difficult to breathe. We digest a torrent of news stories about corruption among the ruling class that goes unpunished. We see media and educational institutions colluding to keep all in blissful ignorance of their servitude. We see the intimidation and outright thuggery practiced by officials from the lowest pencil pusher to the highest elected and unelected men and women. Their arrogance galls us. Their conceit offends us. Their open thievery infuriates us. Their wanton destruction of the future for their present gratification horrifies us.

In response, being people of courage and conviction, we have taken action. We have contacted our elected officials, the ones who are charged with "protecting and defending the constitution," that noble document that so eloquently recognizes our rights and supposedly limits their power. We vote, of course. We have even taken to the streets by the hundreds of thousands in recent years, protesting the most egregious attacks on our freedom. Our calls and letters are ineffective or ignored, our votes, at best, merely exchange one tyrant for another, our mass protests fall on deaf ears. We are left feeling powerless and ineffective in our attempts to protect our liberty and that of future generations.

As all these emotions simmer within our souls, as our flesh chafes from the chains of our growing bondage, most of our fellows remain either blissfully ignorant or unconcerned. As much as we want to grab them and scream, we, for the most part, calmly try to educate and reason with our family and friends. Yet their vacuousness seems impenetrable. Which, while tedious, would be inconsequential except for the fact that these people make up the vast majority of the electorate. The votes of five or ten uninformed, irresponsible morons is more than enough to cancel out the single vote of a passionate patriot..

So we resign ourselves to do the best we can while being ruled by despots voted in by idiots bought off with stolen money and lies. We are admonished to be good losers, work within the system, majority rules, we're all socialists now. Yet deep within us we know that the system is rigged to ensure the two parties share an ever increasing power. A tyranny of the majority is just as immoral as any other tyranny and we are *not* all socialists! And then there is the worst of platitudes-"We get the government we deserve." After all, we voted for it. *I didn't vote for it!* Do I deserve to have my hard earned wealth stolen from me to be given to irresponsible individuals and politically connected fatcats? Do I deserve to be intimidated by countless government agencies and protected union or racist thugs? Do I deserve to be bullied by lawyers, judges and busybodies when I try to exercise my rights to speak and associate freely? Do I deserve to have my person violated in the most intimate fashion just because I want to travel? Do I deserve to be denied medical treatment because it is not cost effective or of a form not approved of by the wise oligarchs who rule? Do I deserve to be put into the straightjacket of government acceptability determined by officials interested only in naked power voted into place by ignorant fools who have relinquished any responsibility for their own lives, eagerly begging for crumbs from the master's table with the stupid grin of loyalty and gratitude displayed by the lowliest and most abused dog?

I don't deserve it, you don't deserve it, no one *deserves* to live under oppression and tyranny. My fellow man through his vote does not have the ability to destroy my humanity without my permission. We are not bound by our ancestor's decisions to embrace tyranny, they cannot do so on behalf of all future generations. No man through force or fraud can reduce me to slavery without my consent. This was the wisdom and the courage of the revolutionary generation. They withdrew their consent from the most powerful empire on earth at the time and in doing so risked their fortunes and lives for the supreme honor of standing as free men. They were a minority who took decisive action, the majority waited on the sidelines in fear, not desiring to risk what little they had and incur the wrath of the powerful. Those determined men of honor and courage were called traitors, fools, terrorists and worse. They were the most dangerous of men for two reasons.

First, they believed that the exercise of their God-given natural rights should not, indeed, cannot, depend upon the good will of the powerful or the courage of their fellow man. Just because the vast majority decide to live in meek, subservient ignorance is no reason for an individual to suffer the indignity and inhumanity of slavery.

Second, neither their fortunes nor their lives were of any consequence compared to living, for however brief a time, as free men.

Part one of what follows is a philosophical, legal and historical justification for individuals who want to take action and reclaim their heritage and natural rights and have the courage to do so in the face of tyranny. Part two is a series of suggestions for taking action both within and outside the tyrannical system. Ultimately, the options available within the system will shrink to nothing as we approach the absolute despotism of a modern totalitarian state in America and perhaps, the world. But we have examples throughout history, including a multitude within our own religious and cultural tradition, to encourage us. For these are universal principles, they apply to every man, everywhere, at every time. Although the United States has a tradition of liberty, when *any* man or woman becomes enlightened to the values of their liberty and humanity, they have the right to live their lives in liberty to the extent of their courage and the depth of their sacrifice. Will liberty, honor and truth always triumph? The honest answer is no. Not every rebellion against tyranny has succeeded. Many have seen their fortunes confiscated, been thrown into prison or have been executed for standing against those who would have them live as slaves. Yet to them liberty was so dear, the hope that their children would not suffer as they did so compelling, that they were willing to use whatever means they had at their disposal in the attempt to restore their dignity as human beings and assure freedom for their posterity.

Since the first man decided to rule over his brethren, mankind has been engaged in an eternal struggle for liberty. The battle is essentially over authority. Does the government have the supreme authority to do whatever it wants or does fundamental authority and sovereignty reside with the individual? The contest, ultimately, comes down to one of force. What happens when the government imposes an unjust requirement or restriction? If you choose to comply, however reluctantly, you are admitting that all authority resides with the government and your own liberty is not worth your words of weak protest. You have extended your hands and allowed the first link in chain of your slavery. By submitting to the first act of injustice, both you and the despot will find further acts of tyranny much easier to accommodate.

As you ponder your current circumstances under a government whose tyranny is becoming ever more blatant, whose destructive tendencies ever more obvious and whose usurpation of power ever more dangerous, you need to ask yourself; how much do you value liberty? Does embracing the risk of fulfilling the destiny for which you were created, to live as a free human being, outweigh the artificial security of submitting to the master's commands? Is the shrinking modicum of comfort we are allotted in exchange for our submission sufficient to suppress your sense of justice and morality? After all, your liberty is only worth the price you are willing to pay for it.

"Tyranny, like hell, is not easily conquered; yet we have this consolation with us, that the harder the conflict, the more glorious the triumph." Thomas Paine

"Resistance to tyrants is obedience to God." Thomas Jefferson

Philosophical Justification

When we consider government, or even our basic interactions with our fellow man, we do so based on a set of principles; ideals and values we have internalized. We have a view of the way things should be in the world and it is our philosophy about the nature of man that determines our outlook and by extension, our actions. Government and society, as formal and informal intercourse among individuals, derive their forms from our collective view of ourselves. A large part of our problem in the West, its cultural decline and the rise of totalitarianism, is the fact that our current worldview is shaped by a relativistic, short sighted and egocentric creed that finds little time for, and no value in, the introspection required to discover the meaningful and eternal values that have positively shaped moral and prosperous cultures in the past, including our own. It was religion and an appreciation for philosophy that have traditionally played the primary role in encouraging individuals to consider and embrace positive and lasting ideals and values, neither of which are held in much esteem in the West any longer.

Since volumes have been written about the nature of man and his relationships with one another, the organization of society and government, I am not going to attempt a lengthy treatise on any of the above. But, in order to figure out why we are in the situation in which we find ourselves, why we are dissatisfied with it, what are the moral actions permissible and required to change it and into what we desire to change it, we must have a reasonable, workable, consistent ethical and philosophical framework from which we can act morally. Therefore, I will focus primarily on the essential nature of man as a free individual, the purpose and scope of government and the interaction between the two.

We must first understand that life, liberty and property existed before the law and government, the law does not create or give value to these things, they exist and have value in and of themselves. Our faculties, the freedom to use them and the right to the results of their application, these make up the essential nature of man. Man is a free standing, independent, individual agent, a sovereign, and his right to act as such are intrinsic to him. This results in several moral assertions. First, no man can assert authority *by right* over another man. Second, no man can claim rights superior in quality or quantity to anyone else. Finally, all human agencies, being constructs of individual sovereigns, can have no claim of authority beyond that available to their creators.

All this being true, whether or not we actually

exercise our sovereign rights to act freely, it is our moral and ethical right to do so. No one and no organization has a moral right to take what, by definition, belongs only to us and is indivisible from our essence as a human beings. The state has no sovereignty over us, they only have sovereignty relative to other states. The state has no rights, only power and authority specifically delegated to it. What, therefore, is the individual's relationship to the state, what constitutes the legitimate authority of the state and what are the limits of our allegiance to the state?

We must first answer the question, what is government? "It is the collective organization of the individual right to lawful defense." (Bastiat) Every individual has a right to defend, with force if necessary, his person, his life, his liberty and his property. The reason men formed government was to collectively defend their individual rights. However, this does not mean that the individual gives up his right to self defense to the collective. I still have the right to use force to protect my person and property against those who desire to rob or kill me. It would be absurd to think I give up my right to use force to fight off an attacker in a dark alley, even using deadly force if warranted, because I have agreed to unite with my fellows for the common defense. If they are not there, must I wait for them? Of course not. I am under no obligation to allow a violation of my person or property because I have entered a cooperative agreement for defense if that cooperative is unable or unwilling to protect me at any one moment. The idea that we relinquish any fundamental right to even a legitimate government is absurd. Our rights to self directed independence, our sovereignty, are not even under our authority, they come, in the words of our founders, from our Creator, and therefore they cannot be surrendered. It is this idea that we must submit to any abuse of our rights because we chose our government or its representatives, that we freely surrender some portion of our sovereignty to the state as a condition of enjoying the collective protection agreed upon, is to mentally and physically cross the line into slavery, it is a denial of our humanity. If a government can convince you that you must give up some sovereignty to participate in the collective, there is no limit to the surrender of rights they will require. A government's assertion of fundamentally illegitimate authority is easy if you are convinced the surrender of your sovereignty and its accompanying rights is not only possible but desirable.

"If men, through fear, fraud or mistake, should in terms renounce or give up any natural right, the eternal law of reason and the grand end of society would absolutely vacate such a renunciation. The right to freedom being a gift of Almighty God, it is not in the power of man to alienate this gift and voluntarily become a slave" Samuel Adams

So what constitutes a legitimate government,

what do we agree to when we enter into this collective agreement for self defense? The law, as the expression of government, is meant to enforce proportional response to any violations of individual rights. Before or outside the law, an individual, family or clan determined the response to an offense and if those retaliated against did not think it appropriate, they would retaliate in turn and much needless blood would be shed in endless feuds. Therefore, we relinquish to government our prerogative to seek justice on our own terms. Because government and its accompanying law are based on the individual right of self defense, it cannot logically, morally or legitimately exceed the bounds of that which it acts as a substitute, namely the individual right of self defense. Since it is immoral for an individual to initiate force against the person, liberty or property of another individual it is immoral for the government to do so as well. Any law that exceeds this right of self defense, if it in any way uses the collective force to offend the person, restrict the liberty or steal the property of any individual who has not done the same to his fellow, it is illegitimate, immoral and unlawful.

If a nation were organized under these moral and legal limitations, the people would be moral, responsible and prosperous. No one would have an argument with government for his person would be respected, his labor and the results of it his own, and his property protected. When successful, no one could credit government and when one fails, no blame could be placed upon the same. We would not constantly bicker over applications of government power for or against our interests. We would not see the inefficient application of labor or capital wrought by government decisions, resources would be allocated according to the efficiencies of the free market. The state would only be felt through the "domestic tranquility" provided for by a government solely concerned with the defense of natural rights. When everyone has the unrestricted use of their faculties and the unencumbered distribution of the fruits of their labor, individual, cultural and social progress will be ceaseless, uninterrupted and unfailing.

Government and law have, of course, gone beyond, *way beyond*, their proper function and it has not done so in debatable and inconsequential matters. Government has always been, and will always be, the greatest threat to the life, liberty and property of man. As soon as it steps beyond its legitimate purpose it begins acting in opposition to its own goals and destroys its own objectives. It annihilates the justice it is charged with maintaining, it destroys the rights it was charged with protecting and respecting. It places the collective force in the hands of those who would use it to abuse and plunder their fellows with the cloak of legality. It turns plunder into a right and lawful defense into a crime. It elevates the basest among us into lauded public servants and labels patriots as terrorists. Immorality is expected and virtue goes out of fashion. When plunder becomes a statutory entitlement and life and liberty are exercised only at the whim of authority, no one respects the life, liberty or property of anyone and the foundation of a just society and a moral culture is destroyed.

It is difficult to conceive of the world our founders envisioned and created for our memories do not go back to a time before we chose to abandon those ideals and began plodding along the road to serfdom. We have been conditioned to accept things as they are and believe they are the way they should be. We accept the premise of government involvement and squabble only over the means and extent. For those who have lost the ability to consider life outside of this paradigm, the concept of liberty is foreign and they will remain content in their servitude.

"When men yield up the privilege of thinking, the last shadow of liberty quits the horizon." Thomas Paine

Legitimate law is fundamental for a just society. The law is justice and government exists only for suppressing injustice. The law, applied equally to all and limited to punishing only real violations of individual rights, will assure the society described above. The law must spell out in clear and plain language for all concerned what the penalties for various violations are. This is the first requirement of legitimate law, that it must be published in a way that it is understood and available to all. When law is concerned only with the actual violation of another's rights to life, liberty and property it is limited, unambiguous and easily understood. This fosters a respect for the law and those charged with its enforcement and mitigates most abuses. This is no longer the case. Congress creates an average of one new crime a week. Federal agencies create thousands more, too many to count. Then add state and local legislatures and regulators and their laws and regulations. The greatest perversion of the law is a preponderance of regulations that no one knows or even has the ability to know. The idea that the state can legislate and regulate everything is the very definition of totalitarianism. Too much law amounts to no law at all. When everyone's behavior is criminalized offenses have no meaning apart from the will of the enforcer. The rule of law devolves into official discretion, the rule of man.

> *In this, our age of Infamy*
> *Man's choice is but to be*
> *A tyrant, traitor or prisoner:*
> *No other choice has he.*
> Aleksandr Pushkin

When everyone is a lawbreaker, enforcement is, by definition, discriminatory. It may be based on race, politics or simple personal animosity. With such a wide variety of offenses to choose from, if the government chooses to do so, it will find something illegal in anyone's life. In fact, it is much easier to prove a procedural offense than an actual criminal one. Al Capone's case may be the most famous in this respect but Martha Stewart and Rodger Clemens are more recent high profile cases. Put such power in the hands of a plethora of regulatory agencies churning out tens of thousands of pages of new rules every year, add an incomprehensible tax code, and finding something criminal isn't difficult. Even worse is without the need for witnesses, it is much easier to concoct or plant evidence (paperwork or drugs) to assure an individual conviction than it would be to plant someone else's actual property (larceny) or contrive an assault.

The second test of legitimacy is that the only way such laws can be justified is if those to whom they apply are the ones who determine their content. If this is done outside a simple democracy, individuals empower their representatives to take up the responsibility for legislation. We delegate to these men authority but that authority cannot exceed that which we freely give or, in the case of our sovereign rights, can give. No legislator has the ability to reduce our sovereignty or our ability to exercise our rights. Any attempt to do so is an illegitimate usurpation of authority and any laws that seek to reduce our sovereignty or natural rights are patently illegal and immoral. As such, we are under no obligation to obey such law or recognize the authority that promulgated it.

Nor can a legislator delegate that authority to another, a premise consistently violated under our current system of legislators passing open and ambiguous laws in which the bureaucratic regulator in an unaccountable agency determines their scope and specific content. We charge our legislators with taking care of our interests within a clearly defined scope of activity. He does not have the authority to delegate that responsibility to another, allowing another carte blanc to use that authority as he sees fit. Such an individual is unaccountable and is free to exercise power indiscriminately. Yet, this is our current situation. Doesn't congress often complain about abuses in regulatory agencies but seems powerless to do anything about it? Even the executive, ostensibly in charge of all these agencies, asserts little control over the middle and lower level bureaucrats who exert wide discretion in the exercise of power. Why must we submit to rule by bureaucrats who constantly manipulate our environment and threaten our well being? They do so in ways that destroy the economy and hence our property not due to decisions we have made but by taking risks on our behalf without our consent. Our elected officials have abrogated their responsibilities and refuse to hold an uncontrollable bureaucracy accountable, putting all of us under bureaucratic despotism, "erecting a multitude of New Offices, and" sending "hither swarms of Officers to harass our people, and eat out of their substance." Such a situation is immoral, as the founders stated in the Declaration of Independence, and we are not obligated to submit to such injustice.

How is it that we, as a nation, a moral people who risked our lives for freedom, have abandoned that freedom and meekly submit to such an immoral system? Bastiat identifies what he calls the fatal flaw of mankind; when they can they wish to live and prosper at the expense of others. For those without the internal moral compass and sense of honor necessary to resist this impulse, legitimate law exists to ensure that submitting to that impulse has consequences that exceed that of honest work. Those whose proclivities tend toward the plunder and abuse of their fellow man will continue as long as plunder is easier than work. The legitimate purpose of the law and government is to protect us from such people and punish their actions.

What then, are we to make of the vast majority of our fellows who either embrace or submit to the depravity of living at the expense of their fellows, who have given such a system their assent, either happily or grudgingly? They are, to put it mildly, of unsound mind. They fall into one of two camps. One, they have, through fear or fraud, chosen to act against their own self interests. They are no different than the followers of Jim Jones, drinking the poisoned kool-aid because they have been convinced it is good for them or there is a gun pointed at their heads. The second group are those who desire to hire the legislator as a mercenary to steal the property of others. They are evil, greedy people and deserve contempt no different than that of the legislator who wields the pen and sword for his own benefit.

This is the defect of democracy; the idea that my liberty is dependent upon the esteem with which the majority of my fellow men hold their own liberty. By what means have we delegated authority to other individuals or groups of individuals to do things against our natural rights they have no right to do? Another person through their vote or our predecessors through theirs have no right assign themselves authority that belongs only to us any more than an individual or group who would seek to usurp that power through force of arms does. A republic such as ours is designed to protect both the rights of the minority from the majority and the majority from a determined minority. Neither a majority or a minority can trample individual rights for rights do not depend on votes, elections, regulations, laws, polls, constitutions or any other man made objects.

"An elective despotism was not the government we fought for." James Madison

So what are our moral obligations under an illegitimate authority that has perverted the law to actually sanction plunder and in which the thieves redefine themselves as public servants whose very reason for existence is to loot and pillage? If an individual has the fundamental right of self defense, including the use of force, against the thief who breaks into his house or mugs him on the street, does he surrender that right to the collective? No, of course not. Even under a just government charged with protecting individual rights, the individual does not relinquish his right, responsibility or obligation to protect his individual person or property. If the collective force, the government, becomes an agent of the thief or a thief itself, passing laws destructive to individual rights and designed to utilize the force of the collective to confiscate the property of the individual, the individual retains the right of self defense against plunder even when the plunder is given the veneer of legality. Plunder is never moral or legal and self defense against it, no matter its source, is moral and justified.

If we do not have the protection of the law, if the laws are immoral and illegal, if they are applied inconsistently and with favoritism by the powerful, if the government is unable or unwilling to fulfill its responsibility or worse, becomes an agent directly or indirectly involved in violating natural rights, the total responsibility for an individual's right of self defense falls back on himself. In the absence of lawful authority, an individual's actions to secure his person or property and to seek justice as an individual are not vigilantism, which is operating outside a legitimate, just, functional system to which he has voluntarily given his consent, but it is acting as a moral individual in an anarchical system just as our distant ancestors did before government.

For an illegitimate government is no different than the "mob", an organized thugocracy which steals with threats of violence. Consider a neighborhood in which a group of thugs demand "protection" money from every business and individual and if that money is not given "voluntarily", harm will come to property or individuals. Is that any different from a government demanding your property and allegiance on threat of fine or imprisonment? If there is no authority in that neighborhood, the police, prosecutor or judges are unwilling or unable to deal with the thugs, or are on their payroll, is it not your right to use whatever means necessary to protect yourself and your property? Wouldn't that also include the right to take action not only against the responsible parties but also to recover stolen property? If they have threatened and used violence, is it not morally justified to visit violence upon them? Would this not apply to a government that engages in the same? Whether voted for or as a consequence of usurpation, I did not, indeed I cannot, relinquish my rights to life and property and therefore my rights to act in defense of my life and property remain with me. I only need choose to exercise them. Will such be called traitors, pirates and revolutionaries or worse? Of course, for the authority will always try to legitimize itself by attempting to delegitimize its opponents.

When this point is reached, where authority becomes illegitimate, prejudicial and destructive, people will naturally rebel against such injustice. This will result in either anarchy or restoration. It will be anarchy if, without a moral compass, each man seeks to plunder what he will and get what he can without respect for his fellow. This is the path of most revolutions. One group of plunderers are exchanged for another as disparate groups vie for control. It will be restoration only if each man respects the rights of his fellows and seeks to establish the rule of justice and new institutions that will best assure his "safety and happiness." This was the path of the American Revolution where the fundamental and controlling ideal was respect for the rights of all, friend and foe alike.

"The danger to which the success of revolutions is most exposed, is that of attempting them before the principles on which they proceed, and the advantages to result from them, are sufficiently seen and understood." Thomas Paine

When most consider, however, what would push us over the edge into revolutionary activity, we think about imminent threats to our life and liberty, of a despotic government rounding people up and sending them to the gulag or lining them up and and shooting them. Of course we would have no problem violently resisting such a regime. Yet the British did no such things to our forefathers to set them on the path of revolution. The fact is the American Revolution was fought over *property* rights. This seems quaint to us today, we are accustomed to government confiscating our property every moment of every day. Among the various assaults on our rights we think that property is the least of them, that to respond to theft with violence is to engage in a disproportionate reaction. *It is not* and our founder's agreed. Taxation, after all, is the state using its monopoly on the use of force to take the property of individuals. To do so without the consent of the property owner is theft. To do so with any aim other than the protection of rights is plunder. Property is essential to freedom. It enables all of us to secure and exercise our natural rights. Without economic freedom personal and political freedom do not exist. Why wouldn't it be proper to react to such theft with violence knowing that it is an assault on life and liberty?

"The moment the idea is admitted into society that property is not as sacred as the laws of God, and there is not a force of law and public justice to protect it, anarchy and tyranny commence." John Adams

Our property is a result of using all our individual faculties in absolute liberty to sustain and enhance our life. An attack on property is an attack on life itself for if our ability to provide for ourselves is diminished, our survival is compromised. Is the theft from the overabundance of a "rich" person the same as stealing bread from the hand of the poor? Is the rich man as justified in defending his abundance as the poor his sustenance? Yes, for both are expressions of their efforts to sustain and enhance their lives and if an individual or government does not value the property of the wealthy, there is no reason to assume they will value the property of the poor. Any statements to the contrary, any appeals to "fairness" or "redistribution" that attempt to justify the "legal" confiscation of the fortunes of the wealthy are merely a pretense to enslave all under the assumption that all property belongs to the state, rich and poor alike, and it is the state's job to determine its use. Therefore no property is respected, of the rich or poor.

It should be clear that acting in opposition, even violently, to a criminal or a criminal government that initiates an assault on our life, liberty or property is morally justified. No individual or corporate entity has the moral right to take those things that are essential to our humanity and we have the right, indeed the duty, to defend ourselves against any attempt, no matter how seemingly insignificant, to reduce our sovereignty, liberty or property.

Legal Justification

The philosophical underpinnings of our nation as eloquently stated in the Declaration of Independence were codified in the Constitution of the United States of America. That document is the supreme law of the land. It was agreed to by "We the People....in Order to form a more perfect Union, establish Justice, insure domestic tranquility, provide for the common defense, promote the general welfare and secure the Blessings of Liberty to ourselves and our Posterity.." It was agreed that this government, laid upon the foundation of the principles they fought a revolution for and by organizing its powers in such a fashion, would "seem most likely to effect their safety and happiness" and fulfill the only moral duty of government, the security of rights.

It was a brilliant document, describing a government of very limited and specific power. Article 5 gave instructions for how *any* changes to those powers were to be made, a very difficult process. In fact, the whole point of this form of government was to assure that it would remain within its bounds and the people would find it easy to keep it there. In order to guarantee that the document was abundantly clear about these powers and the rights of the people the first ten amendments were immediately added, culminating in the ninth and tenth amendments.

"The enumeration in this constitution, of certain rights, shall not be construed to deny or disparage others retained by the people." and *"The powers not delegated to the United States by the Constitution, nor prohibited by it to the States, are reserved by the States respectively, or to the people."*

This means that without the amendment process, the Federal Government has no *legal* right to engage in *any* action or assume *any* power not specifically granted it by the Constitution and, by extension, we the people. It cannot, and with the adoption of the fourteenth amendment the states cannot, pass any law or adopt any power that restricts or diminishes either enumerated or non-enumerated rights held by "the people", you and I as individuals. Any such action is illegal by definition because the "Constitution and (*only*) the laws of the United States *which shall be made in Pursuance thereof...*shall be the supreme law of the land." Article six.

Of course, the government has appropriated powers for itself far beyond those enumerated and we submit to this assault because we have somehow been convinced that the majority of our fellow citizens can vote to surrender all our rights or plunder their fellows. That is the fallacy of a democracy and our nation was *not* set up as a democracy. The Constitution was designed to protect the rights of the individual from the actions of the majority. It was designed to keep government limited to specific tasks and it was explicitly prohibited from making laws that would infringe on the natural rights of its citizens. There is no legal or moral justification for the Federal Government passing *any* law that violates our rights regardless of what the majority wants, what the polls say, what most legislators desire or the executive wills.

"A strict observation of the written laws is doubtless one of the highest duties of a good citizens, but it is not the highest. The laws of necessity, of self-preservation, of saving our country when in danger, are of higher obligation. To lose our country by a scrupulous adherence to written law, would be to lose the law itself, with life, liberty, property and all those who are enjoying them with us; thus absurdly sacrificing the end to the means." Thomas Jefferson

Where did this idea that the Federal Government has the power to regulate every behavior come from? We must go all the way back to the Lincoln-Douglass debates over slavery. Slavery, of course, is the most egregious violation of liberty next to murder and government sanction of it is an abomination. However, the arguments for the

Federal Government intervening in the issue in the territories and the states are the same ones used against alcohol, polygamy, prostitution, drug use, and incandescent light bulbs. It is the argument between localism/individualism and central control. On one side is the belief that different individuals and local jurisdictions (towns/counties/states) should be free to adopt rules and regulations that best suit those local populations as long as those rules do not infringe on the rights of others. Those rules should be adopted and enforced at the local level. On the other side are those who believe that the nation (national government) should make all the rules regarding behavior and moral principles and they should apply to everyone everywhere.

Localism lost because there have always been those who cared about, and therefore sought to regulate, the lives of others beyond their own social circle. Instead of using persuasion and social pressure to convince their fellows not to engage in behavior they found objectionable (drinking, promiscuity, smoking, drug use, sodomy, land use, energy use, etc.), they seek the power of government coercion to achieve their goals. Their knee jerk reaction to any problem is "there ought to be a law..." They believe they are doing this for the good of the society as well as the individual. Instead of the very limited power of the Federal Government and the "live and let live" libertarianism and the belief that free individuals solve problems best which characterized early

Americans concerning their government, we have various vocal minorities convincing politicians eager for their votes and money as well as a politician's desire to be seen as supporting morality or being "enlightened" on certain issues passing laws that constantly infringe on the rights of one group to satisfy the desires of another.

"The invasion of private rights is chiefly to be apprehended, not from act of Government contrary to the sense of its constituents, but from acts in which the Government is the mere instrument of the major number of the Constituents." James Madison

    The major problem here is that once government force is used to regulate one behavior that does not infringe on the rights of another (the creation of victimless crimes, for example), that power can be turned against that group depending on who's in charge. Certainly the Christian moralists who opposed polygamy and prostitution and gave us prohibition would not approve of gay marriage, abortion or the removal of all symbols of their faith from the public square. Yet the same arguments and government machinery are at work.

    Not only has this changed the way we view the government's, particularly the Federal government's, role in our lives, it changed the way the courts view the application of the law. Criminal convictions were once a result of juries determining not only the facts of a case but the *intent* of the accused and the validity and application of the law under which he was accused. Culpable intent, however, is no longer a requirement when it is inconvenient for the government as it goes about achieving the public good. In *United States v. Brilliant* Chief Justice Taft noted this was the case "where the emphasis of the statute is evidently upon achievement of some social betterment rather than the punishment of the relevant crimes." In the case of murder, the state must prove that the perpetrator acted with criminal intent. If not, it is manslaughter or self defense. However, a drug addict with a certain amount of drug on his person can be charged with "intent to distribute" whether he had that intent or not. The vast majority of federal legislation and regulation does not require the government to prove intent to obtain a conviction. In fact, an intent to *comply* isn't even a defense as thousands of people hounded by the EPA, FDA and IRS can attest to.

With a plethora of regulations of which our ignorance is assured, the ease of government convictions due to the lack of having to prove intent, jury review rare and constrained, and courts more than willing to uphold convictions where social goals are at stake, we have a recipe for tyranny. Law can go far beyond moral and constitutional boundaries with impunity.

Who determines whether or not a law exceeds those limits? Most assume that the Supreme Court has the final say but that would mean government authority is defined by an oligarchy of nine supposed infallibles, or even one "swing vote". The Constitution gives them no such power. In fact, the three branches were supposed to be checks on one another yet our misplaced faith in the lie of government's ultimate authority to determine its own boundaries has placed us under tyranny. No, the final authority to determine the limits of the Federal Government are the people themselves who are just as qualified to determine whether or not a law constitutes an assault on their rights as do presidents, congressmen or judges.

"The mass of citizens is the safest depository of their own rights." Thomas Jefferson

Perhaps more so, since legislators seem enamored of considering themselves above the law, geniuses whose civic virtue abrogates the need for regulating their own activities. The fact is that "we the people," as collection of individuals with inalienable rights and fundamental liberty, possess not only the moral, but also the legal authority under the Constitution to reject any legislation or regulation that violates our rights. This is not anarchy, each man picking and choosing which law he chooses to follow at his convenience. Individually, we must make moral and reasoned decisions with fidelity to the concept of natural rights and collectively we have the right of a jury of our peers (6th Amendment) who not only decide guilt or innocence but the validity of the law under which we are charged.

It would also be appropriate to add here that the vast majority of Federal law is not a product of the congress fulfilling the role it was assigned in Article one, section seven, but of innumerable unelected and unaccountable bureaucrats who churn out a thousand pages of new regulations every week, regulations that have the force of law and the ignorance or violation of which can result in excessive fines or imprisonment. These regulations have nothing to do with violations of natural rights but are the product of social and environmental engineers whose sole purpose is to expand the power of government, take more of our money and liberty and mold us into their image. Law created by unaccountable individuals for such purposes is not law at all but a naked exercise of power, it is illegitimate at all levels and can therefore make no moral or legal claim to our loyalty beyond the government's coercive ability.

Of course, I am under no illusion that just because these are the legal facts I have any legal standing that would be recognized by government or even the majority of my fellows who believe otherwise. Those with the gold and the guns make the rules, illegal and immoral though they may be. While it took a long time for despotism to overcome the impediments of such a brilliant document and an informed and independent people who jealously guarded their liberty, all three branches of government have colluded to ignore the clear limitations placed on government authority and have usurped power. Instead of legal justification for their actions, legislators, executives and judges have said that government power is what they say it is, it is limited only by their own discretion. The fact is that we have been living in a post-constitutional country since at least the beginning of the twentieth century, probably since 1861. By reinterpreting or ignoring the limits placed on it by the Constitution for its own benefit, our government has broken the contract "We the People" made and there is, therefore, no "binding legal authority" we have agreed to under which such a government is morally or legally entitled to our fidelity. It is a government of men and not of laws who ensure obedience through deception or fear-tyranny by any definition.

"The evils of tyranny are rarely seen but by him who resists it." John Hay

The Bill of Rights was added to the Constitution because there were those who feared that without unambiguous limitations on government power and explicit enumeration of some of the more fundamental rights, the Federal Government would quickly exceed its bounds as all governments are wont to do. However, to one degree or another, every single one of those guarantees has been ignored by legislators and executives with the complicity of the courts. Volumes have been written about these abuses of power so a few examples of each will suffice. While you may not consider your own rights infringed upon yet, the precedent has been set. The government has not yet chosen to go after everyone it could; making examples of a few is usually sufficient to secure compliance among the rest. Look at how successful the IRS is with this tactic. But be assured, if the government chooses to define you as a threat, it has all the tools it needs to silence and destroy you.

Amendment one:

"Congress shall make no law respecting the establishment of religion, or prohibiting the free exercise thereof; or abridging the freedom of speech, or of the press; or the right of the people to peaceably assemble, and to petition their Government for a redress of grievances."

I am sure you are well acquainted with the long standing war on religions expression on both public and private property and the restrictions on free speech as a result of political correctness that can lead to economic and public recriminations. However, there have been more specific examples of the government ignoring the clear meaning of this amendment. The government has assaulted our right to free speech and the press by fining journalists who publish legally obtained information, fining web site creators who publish "unapproved" content (anti-abortion web site creators, for example), upholding eternal gag orders as in *In re Capital City and Joe Gyan*, removing the public and the press from courtrooms including immigration hearings related to the "war on terror", fining or incarcerating "musicians" for offensive lyrics and suing news outlets that distribute material detrimental to the administration.

Amendment two:

"A well regulated Militia, being necessary to the security of a free State, the right of the people to keep and bear Arms, shall not be infringed."

This enshrined the ultimate right of self defense into the Constitution yet governments at all levels have passed innumerable restrictions (read infringements) on our right to protect ourselves. In some localities it is nearly impossible to even own a gun, much less carry it with you where it will be most effective as a means of protection. Even when the courts actually rule against such laws, governments find a way through fees or other restrictions to accomplish a disarmed populace.

This was also a powerful statement regarding the rights of a state to resist the Federal Government's power. Without a standing army, something the founder's distrusted, the states' militias were the most powerful armed forces in the country and if a struggle for power came down to a question of force, the states would always have the upper hand.

Amendment three:

"No soldier shall, in time of peace be quartered in any house, without the consent of the Owner, nor in time of war, but in a manner to be prescribed by law."

While we don't yet have military troops

utilizing our property without our permission, we are forced to fund, through the confiscation of our property, innumerable agencies and federal law enforcement entities designed to guarantee our subservience.

Amendment four:

"The right of the people to be secure in their persons, house, papers, and effects, against unreasonable searches and seizures, shall not be violated, and no Warrants shall issue, but upon probable cause, supported by Oath or affirmation, and particularly describing the place to be searched, and the persons or things to be seized."

The government now has the ability to access your financial records without warrant under so called "administrative subpoenas" and because the meaning of "financial institution" now includes travel agencies, car dealerships, casinos and their hotels, real estate and insurance agents, lawyers, newsstands, pawnbrokers and the post office, your privacy, the right to be left alone, is gone. The information gathered therein can also be used in ordinary criminal prosecutions. Even evidence obtained during an illegal search is admissible (Pennsylvania Board of Probation v. Scott) for the court stated that the "exclusionary rule" that made such evidence inadmissible in the past (Mapp v. Ohio) isn't a constitutional guarantee and therefore any evidence is admissible if the court says it is. Of course when speaking of illegal searches and seizures, the fact that we are now subject to the most invasive searches imaginable without probable cause just to exercise our right to travel is the most visible assault on liberty in recent years.

Amendment five:

"No person shall be held to answer for a capital, or otherwise infamous crime, unless on a presentation or indictment of a Grand Jury, except in cases arising in the land or naval forces or in the militia, when in actual service in time of War or public danger; nor shall any person be subject for the same offense to be twice put in jeopardy of life or limb; nor shall be compelled in any criminal case to be a witness against himself, nor be deprived of life, liberty or property, without due process of law; nor shall private property be taken for pubic use, without just compensation."

Where to begin with this most important guarantee of our personal liberties against injustice? Under the new rules of the "war on terror" individuals, even American citizens, can be stripped of their rights before any prosecution and declared "enemy combatants." In the case of the "Lackawana Six" in 2003, government lawyers threatened the men charged that if they continued to insist on their due process rights and didn't just plead guilty, they would be declared enemy combatants and without charges or trial, be put into solitary confinement for life.

Also under the "war on terror", an individual may be designated a "material witness" and put into custody indefinitely, Jose Padilla being a notable case. Padilla, when the ability to hold him as a material witness ran thin, was then declared an enemy combatant and put in Defense Department custody. There are countless people being held as enemy combatants who are denied access to lawyers and without trial, without even charges, are being held indefinitely. The government has routinely rejected applications for writs of habeas corpus. It has even used the old soviet tactic of detaining people who criticize government for mental evaluations. Some are terrorists and war criminals, some are not, some are American citizens some are not. Without charges, due process and a trial, rights accorded any human being who has been imprisoned, we do not know and a government that can incarcerate anyone without justification for an indeterminate length of time is the very definition of tyrannical.

When the government desires to assure conviction, law enforcement and prosecutors can lie, deceive, present false promises and coerce individuals in their custody to extract confessions and such confessions are valid (Frazier v. Cupp and United States v. LeBrun). Of course if *you* lie to investigators, even if you are not under oath, you can be prosecuted as the Martha Stewart and Scooter Libby cases revealed. Thomas Coleman, Joe Shapiro, Janet Reno and Paul Rico are among the most well known law enforcement officials engaged in entrapment, witch hunts, torture and, by putting innocent men and women in prison, blatant injustice (often in violation of the eighth amendment). Some of their wrongful convictions have been overturned but there are still innocents languishing in jail, some for life, as a result of their evil actions. If the government decides it wants you, it will go to any lengths to get you.

Through the continual expansion of the eminent domain laws, begun in 1936 in the court of appeals case New York City Housing Authority v. Muller and ending all property rights with the New London v. Kelo case, the court removed any protection of rights or law afforded by the plain meaning of the Constitution. That New York court made the statement that "The law of each age is ultimately what that age thinks should be the law." The court asserted the Constitution only means what our age says it means and this idea has been applied very broadly. The government can now twist any law or prohibition under the Constitution to mean anything in order to assert its power and destroy individual rights. Apart form the courts, bureaucratic agencies have been destroying property rights through regulation so as to render real property unusable and worthless. Of course we cannot neglect to mention the recent Gibson Guitar case where the government raided the facility, seized property yet filed no charges, leaving the company in a legal limbo where it cannot defend itself, as no charges have been filed, yet it cannot recover its property. And should the IRS determine you have failed to comply with some rule or regulation, you can have your property seized or even be jailed without the benefit of a trial before your peers.

Amendment six:

"In all criminal prosecutions, the accused shall enjoy the right to a speedy and public trial, by an impartial jury of the State and district wherein the crime shall have been committed, which district shall have been previously ascertained by law and informed of the nature and cause of the accusation; to be confronted with the witnesses against him; to have compulsory process for obtaining witnesses in his favor, and to have the assistance of council in his defense."

Several egregious violations of this amendment overlap the last but a few more specifics are warranted. If the government wants to bring charges against you it is acceptable for law enforcement to kidnap you and bring you across state lines (Frisbie v. Collins) or from another nation without formal extradition (United States v. Alvarez-Mechain). In fact, the courts have affirmed the concept in the case of Ramizi Ahmed Yosef that the United States has "universal jurisdiction".

The fact is that every day our criminal justice system is corrupted through the practice of purchasing testimony by the prosecution. Witnesses are induced or threatened to testify for reduced sentences, immunity or cash. This is a total perversion of the system for such witnesses are unreliable and can, and have, been induced to say anything so the prosecution can put their targets behind bars. Federal law states that "*whoever* gives, offers or promises anything of value to *any* person for testimony under oath shall be fined or imprisoned for up to two years or both." *Whoever* includes the government but prosecutors are never charged with this routine practice under which anyone in the government's crosshairs could be found guilty. In order to further stack the deck in their favor, the government has been harassing, threatening and jailing lawyers who are trying to represent clients it wants to put away easily. Lynne Stewart, the attorney for Omar Rahman, is a case in point.

Beyond the use of the courts, the government has engaged in direct physical assault on us with impunity. While the BATF, an unconstitutional agency if there ever was one, has been the poster child for lethal government abuse of power for the murders of scores of American citizens under the Clinton administration, and the DEA has assaulted or killed too many innocents making mistakes in the "war on drugs", plenty of other federal agencies have been arming themselves. When even the Department of Education is requesting weaponry for SWAT teams, the government is already way out of control. Only tyrannical governments harass, threaten, kidnap and kill their citizens.

Although not part of the Bill of Rights, the fourteenth amendment, section one, is also relevant to our discussion.

"All persons born or naturalized in the United States and subject to the jurisdiction thereof, are citizens of the United States and State wherein they reside. No State shall make or enforce any law

which shall abridge the privileges or immunities of citizens of the United States; nor shall any State deprive any person of life, liberty or property, without due process of law; nor deny to any person within its jurisdiction the equal protection of the laws."

The authors of this amendment clearly wanted the protections of the Bill of Rights applied to all people, particularly ex-slaves. As we read it, we assume that "due process" refers to several previous amendments and "equal protection" means that not only must the state must treat everyone the same under the law but it must assure justice for all victims regardless of race or class. Our assumptions are wrong.

Almost immediately, the Supreme Court defined the protections under this amendment very narrowly, overturning, for example, the conviction of several men responsible for the murder of blacks in Louisiana (The Colfax Massacre) because the perpetrators were not government officials (United States v. Cruikshank) and even when government officials denied blacks the right to vote (United States v. Reese) they were not held accountable. Part of the argument that carried the day was the statement that "If eight hundred thousand voters (approximate number of voting age blacks in the south at the time) cannot secure the rights to which they have been declared entitled, then it is the best argument that they are not worthy of them."

This has not changed nearly as much as you may think. Cases decided within the last thirty years have confirmed the court's narrow application of this amendment. For example, police forces can enforce drug laws in black neighborhoods but not white ones (United States v. Armstrong 1996), prosecutors and judges can punish crimes that victimize whites more severely than ones that victimize blacks (McClesky v. Kemp 1987) and law enforcement can ignore violent felonies for any or no reason at all without being held legally accountable (Castle Rock v. Gonzales 2005). While these cases emphasize the racial component of legally acceptable discrimination, the fact that we already see politically motivated discrimination of a similar type demonstrates that whenever discrimination is acceptable in government, it can be turned on anyone or any group. It merely depends who is in control of the levers of power.

It is crucial to understand the significance of the examples given above. Society, the people, grant government the exclusive authority to use force to carry out its tasks. The only task that morally justifies the use of force is the collective defense of individual rights. If it uses that force in ways that deprive citizens of their life, liberty or property unjustly, individuals in that government are to be held accountable by the people through the courts. However, if the government can deprive you of life, liberty or property without giving you access to the courts, a review of the charges by your peers or access to counsel, what options remain to you? If you are granted access to the courts but the prosecution can assure a conviction by purchasing testimony, or otherwise tilts the table in their favor, how can you protect yourself? If you have become a target for whatever reason and after the government fails to obtain a conviction in one case, it files another and another and another, using is unlimited resources to overwhelm you, what chance do you have? Are we obligated to subject ourselves to a system of over regulation in which our defense against enslavement is made nearly impossible? If we are not given the opportunity for redress with the legal means provided us is it unreasonable to resort to extra-legal means to protect ourselves? I think not.

Consider where this is leading us. For those that know history, you may be aware that the constitution of the Soviet Union contained many of the protections afforded by our own. Certainly those who love liberty view Stalinist Russia as the very antithesis of a free country and rightly so. Yet we have become very like our old Cold War adversary. The individual protections enshrined in our Constitution are routinely ignored. Extensive surveillance of the population is routine as are informants, even among our children. Our prison population, as a percentage of the population, exceeds that of Stalin's gulags. In fact, Marx, Lenin and Stalin would find much to admire about the current state of our country.

In considering resisting the immoral abuses of power our government routinely engages in, we can do so with the conviction that we are doing so within the framework of the Constitution and the legal framework the founders established. Certainly our arguments will not be recognized by the authorities oppressing us but we can can be confident that we hold both the moral and legal high ground.

Historical Justification

History and mythology provide innumerable examples of individuals and groups who tried, with varying degrees of success, to defend their natural rights against tyranny. The history of mankind, and America in particular, is replete with examples of individuals and small groups, real or imagined, who stood up to entrenched injustice and despotism, sometimes against very long odds and often violently, because they believed that living as free men and women was worth whatever sacrifices they were forced to make. Religious traditions, ballads, plays, music and movies have enshrined the nobility of such courageous and defiant acts in our collective psyche. The reason for this is because we were created to be free, we have an innate sense of justice and morality that provokes us to hate the evils of tyranny and admire those who resist it.

Americans in particular have a national culture that is founded on and encourages these inherent principles and they motivated our forefathers to take the actions that led to the American

Revolution. We are, after all, the children of those men who took extraordinary measures in defense of their God given natural rights. Looking back from our vantage point in which governments, including our own, have assumed and exercised a totalitarian control King George and Parliament could never have dreamed of and confiscate wealth on a scale unimaginable in the eighteenth century, the violent protests of the colonists over a few "consumer" taxes seems quaint and perhaps a bit extreme. It was not to them, obviously, and we can learn much from their example. They understood that taxes are a means of control and the exercise of government control always comes at the expense of liberty. They correctly believed that paying the taxes they knew were intended to subjugate them would be cooperating with their enslavers. They understood the "slippery slope"; if one offense was permitted, the precedent was set for an ideology of encroachment that ends only with slavery, a term they often used when describing England's end game. Unlike our forefathers, we have allowed one assault on liberty after another to be met with nary a whimper and we find ourselves in increasingly tight restraints. Our revolutionary forefathers have given us an example of how to fight tyranny, a tyranny succeeding generations neglected to oppose.

    These men of the revolution used *any and every means* at their disposal to combat an encroaching despotism and make it perfectly clear to England that they were not going to submit to *any* assault on their natural rights. What should be obvious in this case, and any case of protest, are that such activities are a grim game of chicken played between protestors and government. The government seeks some new power and the people protest. The government moves to assert its authority and justify its usurpation. The people rebel. At any point in this deadly contest, one side will capitulate. If the government does, the people retain their rights and freedom. If the people give in they consign themselves to a steadily encroaching tyranny. Once one right or liberty has been surrendered, no good case can be made against abrogating others, the powers of tyranny have set a precedent not easily overturned. If neither side is willing to submit, the government will, at some point, resort to force and the people will have no choice but to respond in kind. The colonists understood the end game which is why their protests moved rapidly along the continuum of justifiable responses.

Finally, consider what kind of men and women these were. In New England, the epicenter of the revolution, they were descendants of the Puritans, religious men and women, many of them preachers or students of divinity. They were moral and religious people who were not shy about putting their struggle in Christian, religious, terms. They engaged in what many would today call decidedly "un-Christian" behavior. We have been steeped in a culture of non-violence, one of the great paradoxes of an American culture that holds the right to keep and bear arms in such high esteem. The colonists did not have such philosophical encumbrances and in some cases one could argue that violence was anything but a last resort. These men understood that any assault on liberty and rights was an assault on life itself and measured responses are inadequate and merely embolden those who hold liberty in contempt.

A review of their responses to several actions by Britain in the decade before the Declaration of Independence will suffice. The Sugar Act of 1764 was the first major attempt by Parliament to tax and control the colonists. Smuggling to avoid taxes was routinely practiced in America and this included the bribing of customs officials. To many this was a reasonable business decision as it was cheaper to pay bribes than to pay duty. It was also, to some degree, a principled response to the belief that commerce and hard work should not be subject to taxation and regulation. We all resent taxes we know are going into the coffers of a corrupt government passing and enforcing laws against our own best interests and the colonists were no different.

There were varied responses to this Act that ranged from civil disobedience to violence. Some of the less "extreme" responses included refusing to provide pilots for navy ships and the harassment of press gangs and other officials. On the other hand, there were more "pointed" protests. George Spenser, an informer in New York, was arrested, paraded through the streets while being pelted with filth, jailed and released on the condition that he leave town and never return. In Newport John Robinson, a customs official, seized the *Polly*, a ship he believed to be engaged in smuggling, in Massachusetts. While Robinson was rounding up a prize crew to sail her to Rhode Island, a "mob" stripped the ship of her cargo, rigging, anchors as well as anything else of value and sank her. The owners then sued the Crown for the loss. Property seized as a result of an unjust law was recovered.

Moral and legal justification for defying the act of the King and Parliament continued to develop as a result of the Two Penny Act, a form of wage and price controls. Patrick Henry boldly stated that the "King, by disallowing acts of this salutary nature, far from being the father of his people, degenerates into a tyrant, and forfeits all rights to his subject's obedience." This was recognized at the time for what it was, a statement of treason against the king.

Things really began to heat up in response to the Stamp Act of 1765. This was another tax on commerce imposed by a far off, unaccountable power. In Boston opposition was led by the "Loyal Nine," who would soon become the "Sons of Liberty." These men chose to meet this assault on their liberty with a violent assault of their own. The goal of their action was to force those commissioned to carry out the Act to resign. After all, if no one was available to distribute the stamps, the act would be unenforceable and, therefore, inconsequential. The protestors did this through intimidation. They began with effigy hangings to make their disapproval unambiguous. If this didn't work, they went to the homes of the offending individuals and destroyed their property. It was specifically targeted to the personal property of the offender, these were not random acts of violence and rioting. In one case they found the official lived in a rented home and the protesters therefore refrained from destroying the property because the owner was not responsible for the official's actions. Of course there were threats against the persons involved but no one was attacked or injured, although there was no question they feared for their lives. In one case when the sheriff showed up and they took up arms and ran him off.

These actions were repeated in other colonies. In Georgia, North Carolina, New York, New Jersey, New Hampshire and Rhode Island, the pattern of coercion and violence was well enough established that most stamp distributors didn't even attempt to fulfill their commissions and resigned. These were not isolated responses but neither were they the majority response. Whether the majority approved or not had no bearing on the legitimacy of their actions. If only a handful had engaged in these activities they would have been justified in defending their own liberty.

Similar actions were taken in response to the Townshend Acts which were taxes on several consumer products including lead, glass, and tea. One of the responses to both taxes was non-importation, basically a boycott on goods from

England, and in some cases, exports to Great Britain. The colonists learned to make their own products, support local craftsman or do without. They also made life difficult for those who rejected this agreement. Of course, many officials were intimidated into resigning and there were even threats of kidnapping of the more notorious and recalcitrant.

To enforce the Acts of Navigation and curtail smuggling, the Royal Navy assigned the *Gaspee* to Rhode Island waters. After seizing several small craft, the captain found himself threatened with arrest by the sheriff. In the course of his duties, the captain eventually ran the *Gaspee* aground where it was boarded by local citizens by force and burned to the waterline. The captain was then arrested by the sheriff and returned to England after paying a huge fine. Local colonial officials, even if they uncovered the names of those responsible for the arson, declined to establish their guilt. This was a case of using local law enforcement sympathetic to liberty to confront and even arrest officials of the powers offensive to liberty while protecting those engaged in acts to protect freedom.

I would be remiss in adding that in addition to all these rebellious activities the colonists were sending petitions and representatives, including the notable Benjamin Franklin, to Parliament and the king. They met with little success and it was his final public humiliation at the hands of the ministry that turned Franklin to the "Glorious Cause." In fact John Adams did not believe reconciliation was possible because the King, parliament, the administration and the electorate "have been now for many years gradually trained and disciplined by Corruption" and concluded that "the Cancer is too deeply rooted, and too far spread to be cured by anything short of cutting it off entire."

The response to the Tea Act of 1773 is probably the most famous. In this case the colonists had no problem going after merchants who cooperated with England in this Act and its primary beneficiary, the East India Company. The most famous action was the Boston Tea Party in which a cargo of tea was taken from the *Dartmouth* and dumped into Boston harbor. In other ports up and down the coast, consignees were "persuaded" to resign their commissions. It was in Quaker Pennsylvania where things were most "persuasive" however. In this case the "Committee for Tarring and Feathering" threatened to practice the same on any pilot who assisted tea ships in the Delaware River. Captain Ayres of the *Polly*, a ship carrying tea, was threatened with the same and sailed for home without attempting to land his cargo. The colonists had no trouble destroying the property of, and threatening physical harm to, those private individuals and businesses cooperating with and benefiting from a law meant to effect their subjugation.

Britain decided to up the ante after this and force the colonists to recognize their authority to pass and enforce any act they chose. Upon the rumor that England was sending troops to force compliance with the Acts every household was urged to arm itself. It was at this time independence was floated as a serious response, at least in Massachusetts. When the troops arrived in Boston, the people made it as difficult as possible for them, refusing to be complicit in their own domination. They refused to pay to house the soldiers, a tax protest of sorts. When a warehouse or other space opened up, a group of families immediately moved in, refusing to leave; acts of civil disobedience. The troops restricted freedom of movement and assembly and the people of Boston, when challenged by a soldier, met his challenge with silence, a consistent application of non-compliance. The courts were also used against the solders as a means of harassment. If they were accused of some civil offense that brought them before a civilian court they were jailed and fined. When legislative bodies were disbanded by royal governors, they reconvened elsewhere even under threats of criminal action. They eventually took over as legitimate authorities alongside the still existent royal authorities.

In April 1775 the British attempted to arrest the ringleaders of the rebellion in Massachusetts and seize the arms that conferred upon them the ultimate ability to defend themselves from tyranny. The colonists gathered in their own defense leading to the battles of Lexington and Concord and the "shot heard round the world". In May Ethan Allen, Benedict Arnold and the Green Mountain Boys seized Fort Ticonderoga, certainly not a defensive action. They did so for the arms it contained, cannon and mortars, and to prevent it from being used as a conduit for British forces from Canada. In June the battle of Bunker Hill was fought for control of the heights around Boston to make the British uncomfortable there and perhaps persuade them to leave, an attempt to liberate Boston.

In the summer of 1775 the continental congress made preparations for the national defense, appropriating money for arms, and choosing George Washington to organize an army. In December 1775 Benedict Arnold invaded Canada and a few months into 1776 George Washington drove Howe from Boston by setting artillery up on Dorchester Heights. That summer the Declaration of Independence was signed.

Even before the Declaration both sides understood the nature of the conflict. Lord North defined the dispute thus; "We are now to dispute whether we have, or have not, any authority in that country." According to an anonymous New Yorker, the British ministry "are bent on the establishment of an uncontrollable authority over the property of Americans." The colonists decided to refuse to recognize Britain's authority and establish their own. This begs the question; Did the signing of the Declaration of Independence confer legitimacy upon the actions of the colonists, past and future? Of course it did not in the eyes of Britain or they would have withdrawn their troops and let the colonists establish a government better able to "secure their safety and happiness." Were the colonist's defense of their rights in Lexington and Concord less legitimate because they happened before the Declaration was signed? How about the offensive actions in Ticonderoga or Canada? What about the tea party or the acts of intimidation? Does the Declaration, or any piece of paper no matter how eloquent or justified confer legitimacy on such activities, or is there something else?

First and foremost, legitimacy is a product of morality. Any endeavor or cause must be a moral one and when we are talking about society the only moral endeavors are those which have as their goal the protection of God given natural rights and the principles of liberty. However, liberty is only worth what you are willing to pay for it. Ultimately, everything in the world comes down to the use of force. Therefore, legitimacy is conferred by two things; morality and force. Force without morality is tyranny, morality without force makes for cowardly slaves. The history of mankind is a never-ending contest between the forces of despotism and the defense of natural rights. Freedom is the possession only of those who are willing to go to *any* lengths to defend their rights as men. Slavery under totalitarianism is the fate of those who either fear the loss of the morsels that remain to them from the tables of their masters or have been brainwashed into accepting their chains in the belief that their restraints are necessary and beneficial. You only have liberty if you are willing to use force to secure it. Our forefathers understood this principle, embraced it and had the courage to put it into action, responding clearly and decisively to the smallest provocation. Most Americans, languishing in ignorant servitude, don't understand it. Of those who do, rare are those with the courage to act decisively. Until we embrace the moral fact that "it is their right, their duty, to throw off such government" that "evinces a design to reduce them under absolute Despotism" we are condemned to suffer its indignities.

A Plan of Action

Filled with a burning conviction about the pervasive tyranny under which we live and the inspired example of our forefathers, an acute need to take immediate action to restore our lost liberty is a natural reaction. Frustration will lead to either resignation or passionate activity. The former are lost, the latter need to be focused effectively. This was the difference between the "mob" of the Sons of Liberty and the mobs of today. The former was focused and the latter indiscriminate. Rioting, looting and wanton destruction most often harms the victims of oppression, further diminishing their condition and turning them against their would be liberators. Such activities are not only counterproductive but wrong, the very antitheses of charity, honor and respect for the natural rights and liberties of our fellow man. Passion must be subject to self control, natural law and common sense.

There are several steps along the road to revolution, often overlapping, and many courses of action are available depending on circumstances and individual capacity. The foundation of it all, however, is knowledge. Knowledge of yourself, your constitution, your nature and your liberties. Knowledge of the Constitution and law. Knowledge of the assaults on your rights and the avenues available for defending them. Knowledge, however, is only the beginning. There are many places to go for knowledge, many articulate defenders of freedom. We must, however, be careful with both sources and volume. With 24/7 news from a variety of sources and viewpoints, the race for ratings often comes at the expense of accuracy. It is easy to become overloaded and overwhelmed, the constant parade of injustice and corruption paralyzing us with an avalanche of targets demanding action and desensitizing us to the continual and flagrant assault on our freedom. If we become well informed but take no action, we merely become educated slaves. Some of our sources, while apparently passionate for freedom, speak in platitudes and generalities, overload us with information, encourage us to accept the premises of our oppressors (some redistribution is acceptable and necessary) or worse, try to restrict our options, ensuring the despots have nothing substantial to fear.

Those who encourage us to action often do so with meaningless admonitions to "get involved" and "stand up". To do what? Work for the two political parties that have sold us into slavery? Vote? Our votes are canceled out by the ignorant or the purchased. Call our elected officials? What incentive do they have to listen to us if the ignorant and purchased keep electing them? Protest? Only to be ignored? Petition? Only to have some judge overturn our decisions? While there are occasional small victories, they are merely speed bumps in the relentless march of tyranny, cultural rot and economic insanity. When push comes to shove with our government, when the daily assault on our liberties shows up on our front door, have these so called defenders of freedom neutered us with unwarranted restrictions on our responses? Are we not going to back down, meekly submitting to injustice, allowing them to take our property or liberty without a fight? While we are supposed to be standing up we back down every day we submit to this unjust and immoral system. It is time we stood up and did that which will actually restore our freedom. The question is, how far are you willing to go when you say you will not back down? Property? Liberty? Life?

This is not to say we should not be politically involved. It is an essential part of an overall strategy. We need to vote and encourage others of like mind to do so. We need to support candidates we know are going to dismantle the system so offensive to our liberty and if none are available, run for office ourselves. We need to continue to try to inform and cajole our current elected officials through our letters, calls and protests. We all know that and have done it. More is required.

Working within and using the system

First and foremost, we must have the right

mindset. If we are looking to a political savior, someone who will come in and "fix" things, we are looking in the wrong place. It is not our political process defines and fulfills our dreams, our dreams are our own. Their fulfillment is our own responsibility. Without the arbitrary restraints imposed by a tyrannical government, it is we, as individuals, who determine how high we rise, how far we go and what we can become as individuals and as a society.

We need to become as isolated from the tentacles of government as possible. If you are dependent on government for your basic needs not only are you enjoying the benefits of stolen goods but you have voluntarily placed yourself under their control. If you have voluntarily placed your life, liberty and property under governmental control, your protests against the same are the height of hypocrisy. You have denied your own rights and your own humanity. How can you effectively protest against a government when it has the power to deny you food, housing, health care or a means of living? Will that fear not paralyze you and curb your action? Of course, the government needs only make a few public examples among its dependents to silence the rest.

It is not only a moral imperative but self sufficiency is necessary to assure our survival when the government is not only unwilling but unable to fulfill the promises it has made with plundered goods and fiat currency. To have a supply of food, water, guns and ammunition and alternate means of communication are only common sense precautions against any disaster, natural or man made. Getting out of debt and securing a steady income will provide greater security and freedom. Moving to a location where liberty is held in higher esteem and the opportunities for legal theft are minimally disruptive reasonable steps. These are all common sense lifestyle choices that promote liberty.

These preparations for personal protection are becoming more crucial as our society slides ever further into immorality and chaos because of, and with the help of, our government. Not only is a criminal system breeding villainy, the government is encouraging racial and class hatred among us. They do this not only for votes but to misplace blame, taking the focus for failure off themselves. This is resulting in individual and mob violence against individuals and groups because of their race or wealth. Through its statements and action, or lack thereof, the government is protecting and encouraging certain racist, union and economic groups to become more violent. The theater for these violent activities has expanded beyond specifically political venues and now encompasses the routine activities of our everyday lives. We must now consider very real threats to our personal safety not only from criminals but from those motivated to violence by our own government and we must take the steps necessary to protect ourselves and our families.

Next, in order to ensure "the security of a free

State," organization is required.

> *"Private associations whose magnitude may rivalize and jeopardize the march of regular government may become necessary in the case where the regular authorities of the government combine against the rights of the people, and no means of correction remains to them but to organize a collateral power which, with their support, might rescue and secure their violated rights."* Thomas Jefferson

It is crucial to have the means of mutual support for the one thing a tyrannical government fears more than anything is organized and determined resistance. It isn't hard to pick off isolated individuals but coordinated groups with established methods and contingencies are another matter entirely. You need to connect with like minded people in your area. Internet "friends" spread across the country aren't going to be much help when government agents come to your door. It is your neighbors, people you know and trust, who will be the most help in dire situations, be they natural or man made. Get a copy of *Citizen Soldier* by Robert Bradley and connect with like minded active or retired military personnel if at all possible. There are a number of organizations of constitutionally committed public safety and active/retired military groups out there today. If you know few of your neighbors, start a neighborhood watch and/or a political discussion group or book club and develop it from there. People are hungry for answers and the security that comes with a plan.

Organization for the common defense against a despotic regime, however, must be undertaken with the utmost discretion. You are, after all, behind enemy lines and facing an adversary with limitless resources to gather information on you and your activities and use that information to harass, intimidate and eventually, if they so choose, take your life, liberty or property. Organizing with your friends, even calling it a militia, is not illegal but if it becomes widely known, you will invite unwanted attention and scrutiny. Therefore, your means of communication and assembly should take into account the fact that the government can and may be listening in on Internet and cell phone communication. Our government has developed extremely sophisticated technology enabling them to track and listen in on terrorist activities around the globe. Do not think that they have not and will not apply that technology to individuals and groups it has already labeled domestic "terrorists."

Finally, know the law. This is considerably more difficult because the government has made the law deliberately confusing in content and overwhelming in volume. They have, however, sometimes attempted to adhere to the strict meaning of the Constitution while using obfuscation and misconception to give them the appearance of authority where none exists. These often revolve around questions of jurisdiction and application. This is no where more apparent than in that most visible and hated instrument of our oppression, the Internal Revenue Code.

The forcible confiscation of the products of our labor is immoral. It is, plain and simple, theft. It is also unconstitutional. "No Capitation, or other direct, Tax shall be laid, unless in Proportion to the Census of Enumeration herein before directed to be taken." (Article 1, Section 9) The Sixteenth Amendment did not change or repeal this section. In fact, income taxes themselves, since their inception during the Lincoln administration, have always been taxes on privileged activity, not on private sector receipts for work. However, by using common terms and giving them legal meanings often contrary to their popular usage, encouraging myths that corroborate public perception and developing a reputation for ruthless enforcement, the government intimidates all of us into voluntarily funding our own enslavement. Erroneously collected income taxes, including FICA and Medicare taxes which are also based on "earnings" make up over half of the Federal Government's income. If Americans began following the law instead of participating in the scheme, we could defund the beast, starving it of the nourishment it requires to enslave us. Individually, you will have the satisfaction of knowing your hard earned money is no longer going to causes you disagree with, bad investments, support for the lazy and irresponsible and an increasingly pervasive regulatory cage.

"To compel a man to furnish contributions of

money for the propagation of opinions which he disbelieves is sinful and tyrannical" Thomas Jefferson

For an exhaustive explanation of this plan of action get a copy of *Cracking the Code* by Peter Eric Hendrickson or go to www.losthorizons.com. This is only one example, albeit a central one. Certainly there are more examples of law and its attendant regulations written in ways to confuse, appropriate authority and assume jurisdiction where none exists. It will take an army to go through so much law but you can unearth those which subject you to the most discomfort and share your findings with others.

Open Defiance
There are, of course, plenty of laws that are openly immoral and unconstitutional, blatant assaults on our liberty. How we handle these will begin to take us well outside our comfort zone. However, the cry of "I will not comply!" by every patriot is the first step in recovering lost liberty. You will be engaging in moral but illegal behavior and the risk of fine or imprisonment is real. This does not necessarily need to be the case. We do have options within the system that will preclude such results.

The first is the time honored tradition of jury nullification.

"I consider trial by jury as the only anchor ever

> *yet imagined by man, by which a government can be held to the principles of its constitution. "*
> Thomas Jefferson

This has gotten a bit of a bad name since the OJ Simpson trial but it is a potent tool for checking the power of government imposition upon us. In fact, judges and juries once had a lot more discretion before the law became so procedural, expansive and detailed. This is a case of "we the people" exercising our authority to determine the morality or Constitutionality of a law as well as the intent and guilt of the defendant. This requires two things. First, non compliance by the offender that will lead to a trial and second, an informed jury. Generally one cannot expect even the majority of a jury to be well informed about Constitutional matters and natural rights but it only takes one. That one could be you.

The second is encouraging your local and state authorities to defy any unconstitutional actions by the Federal Government and to preserve individual liberty. This has become known as "Nullification". Because you will have more success on the local level sooner we will start there. Your local mayor, town and county councils need to be encouraged to pass laws and resolutions in opposition to any federal or even state mandates that would infringe on individual liberty and property rights. The sheriff is key to this plan. You need to elect a sheriff who takes his oath to defend and protect the Constitution very seriously and there are support organizations springing up among sheriffs and law enforcement personnel to encourage this attitude and the corresponding behavior. As the chief local law enforcement officer and therefore the primary custodian of legitimate force, he has the discretion and obligation to use that force in a moral fashion. Some sheriffs have begun using that authority to harass and threaten federal agents trying to enforce unconstitutional law. To take it a step further, to actually arrest federal officers and place them in jail would require local judges who also understand the Constitution and are willing to defy federal authority. This requires political action on a local level, electing judges, legislators and law enforcement officials with courage and knowledge of the Constitution and natural rights.

    This can be taken to the state level as well. We have seen some of this in the last few years with the states passing laws to protect property as a result of the Kelo decision and defiant responses to Obamacare. The problem with all these actions is that both local and state governments are dependent, just as many individuals are, on government largess. To make nullification truly effective, the states must recover their sovereignty and that requires their ability to act autonomously apart from all the rules, regulations and restrictions that come with federal money.

Active Rebellion

    Since the end of World War Two civil disobedience has become the accepted method of protest in the West. Pacifism and peaceful protest may be admirable philosophies and methods but an uncompromising adherence to them will lead to slavery and death in the face of a determined despotism. Such ideals only work if those in authority have a conscience or some respect for human rights and life. It did not work in the Soviet Union or its satellites, it has not worked in communist China, it would not have worked in Nazi Germany, it did not work in Libya or Syria. In such places the evil brutality of the government and its leaders was revealed and there was no possibility they were not going to react violently to any defiance of their authority. When fear is the foundation, courage must be annihilated swiftly and completely. Therefore, I do not consider myself under any obligation to submit to intimidation, beatings, incarceration or murder for an ultimately unworkable ideal.

"The tree of liberty must be refreshed from time to time with the blood of patriots and tyrants. It is its natural manure." Thomas Jefferson

The brutal fact of the world we live in is this. Lack of compliance with tyranny must lead either to armed conflict or surrender. It is a game of chicken in which the action escalates until one side backs down. If it is the government, liberty will win. If it is the people, tyranny will result. We all know that but somehow it has become a bumper sticker idea with no real application. The right to keep and bear arms is a hallowed tradition in America. We know that the second amendment recognizes our right to use deadly force, for what are firearms but lethal force, to defend our lives, liberties and property not only against individual criminals but a criminal government. The founders set up the system so the balance between a limited government and an armed populace would always tip in favor of the people, providing the ultimate check against tyranny.

"No free man shall ever be debarred the use of arms. The strongest reason for the people to retain the right to keep and bear arms is, as a last resort, to protect themselves against tyranny in government." Thomas Jefferson

However, somehow we have gotten it into our collective heads that shooting an armed thug trying to take our wallet in a dark alley is different than shooting a government thug trying to take our life savings. Many of us will fight for the right to carry in the unlikely case of the former but do not even consider it reasonable or possible in response to the daily assault we are subject to from the latter. What is the purpose of the second amendment if it is a threat we are not prepared to follow through on, if it is a right we have no intention of exercising? If we have been conditioned to *never* consider meeting a violent oppression with a reciprocal violent response, we may as well not even have a means of self-defense. If we allow our government propaganda to convince us that it is never proper to react violently to that government's usurpation of power and assault on our rights, we may as well not be armed at all. Stalinist Russia, Nazi Germany or Communist China did not have a tradition of an armed populace and so oppression was easier for there could be no stiff or deadly resistance. If, however, amidst all our tough talk, we would not really consider meeting government force with force of our own, if we have not truly considered where the line is over which our government steps at its imminent *physical* peril, our subjugation is assured. Any resistance will be inconsistent, sporadic and ineffective.

The use of force, however, is a most sober decision. It is easy to talk about government as an impersonal entity that exercises despotic control as if it were an imperious edifice populated by unfeeling machines. It is not. Until the machines take over in some fantastic contrivance like the *Terminator* or *Matrix* movies, government consists of individual people who believe what they are doing is right. In the case of a tyrannical government, they believe in using force to intimidate, plunder and enslave their fellow man. Whether they do it because they enjoy exercising power for its own sake or believe in using force to mold others according to their utopian vision, every individual in such a government has chosen to participate in, and benefit from, an evil system. These individuals are tainted with evil and will continue to participate until a life of plunder becomes either morally unacceptable to them or too socially or physically uncomfortable.

Rebellion against such injustice takes one of two forms. The first, and unfortunately by far the most common, is that the victims desire to become plunderers themselves. This is why most revolutions devolve into chaos and evil; because those involved are only interested in power and revenge. Indiscriminate mob violence, paranoia and widespread suffering and death are hallmarks of such revolutions. For the vast majority of people it is exchanging one tyranny for another. For the victim of plunder and evil to use his victimhood as an excuse to lash out against his fellows who have done him no wrong is to become the evil as well.

However, a rebellion choosing to utilize force to defend lives, property and natural rights, recover stolen property or in response to intimidation, must do so in a manner that is just, targeted and proportional. This is where men and women of honor must exercise their greatest restraint and judgment. Our proportional responses should always err on the side of mercy while still assuring that our point is made. Indiscriminate violence against civilians, even though their stupidity and ignorance have put us in our current position, is not only counter productive but wrong. The attack on the Murrah Federal building in Oklahoma City for example, even in response to the murder of

American citizens, was wrong because it was not aimed at the perpetrators but against those who had no involvement and innocents. It is the individual government officials who intimidate, plunder or otherwise perpetrate the evils of tyranny who are legitimate targets.

Specifically, who are legitimate targets of intimidation and, when necessary, violence? Anyone who participates in an unjust law through its development, adoption or implementation. Every one of them is involved in attacking the life, liberty or property of another unjustly. The phrase "I was just following orders" or "I was only upholding the law" is no excuse. If we can be found guilty and fined or imprisoned in our ignorance of an unjust law or regulation, it is more than reasonable to hold such participants accountable even if they do not have the philosophical insight necessary to recognize the wrong they are participating in. If they have lost the ability to see the theft or assault as wrong, or if they lack the courage to refuse to enforce an unjust law, they are culpable and one should feel no remorse in defending oneself against them to any extent.

"The trade of government has always been monopolized by the most ignorant and the most rascally individuals of mankind." Thomas Paine

In addition to those directly responsible for attacking our liberty and plundering our wealth there are those who directly benefit from collusion with the corruption. Attacks on liberty are only the result of force, no individual or corporation has the ability to force you to give up your wealth or liberty. Only government, with its monopoly on the use of force, can compel you to behave in a certain ways or steal your money. However, those individuals or businesses who are *direct* recipients of stolen funds as a result of collusion with the powerful, receiving favoritism, loans, or direct benefits from government are also legitimate targets.

Ultimately, there are three possible outcomes when the conflict between individual liberty and tyranny reach the point where that conflict turns violent. The first is that the government backs down, repealing all offensive legislation and recognizing the rights of the individual as superior to the state. This is the least disruptive, leaving the familiar forms of government in place, merely constraining it to legitimate activities. Of course those original forms must be conducive to liberty, one cannot hope to rehabilitate a naturally oppressive form of government. Although it sounds unlikely, it did happen in the early stages of our contest with Britain with their repeal of several acts and taxes. However, such a moves on the part of the government are usually pragmatic and do not signal the necessary ideological shift. Without vigilance, the state will try other avenues to assert its illegitimate authority a soon as it believes it has the strength to do so.

The second is an actual civil war in which both sides fight for control of the seat of power. In such a contest, the government seeks to retain its power and the forms of its assertion while the people are seeking "to institute new Government, laying its foundation on such principles and organizing its powers in such form, as to them shall seem most likely to effect their Safety and Happiness." Civil war is the most widespread and destructive form of rebellion and should only be engaged in when those in power prove truly intractable. When this is the only option remaining, hostilities should be primarily focused on those responsible, the "head of the snake" so to speak, in order to keep its duration to a minimum.

Finally, for those who desire to be left alone, secession from the larger body politic would seem the most reasonable course of action. This is fundamentally what our founders did. They had found a place where the vast majority wanted to be governed under different forms than those imposed by Great Britain. They did not want to take control of parliament or replace the king, they merely wanted those powers to leave the colonies, allowing them to govern themselves. Secession is the ultimate form of corporate self determination and as such is the most reasonable and moral resolution to the problem of a consistently oppressive and incorrigible government. In the United States where ostensibly sovereign political entities already exist and there is an increasing polarization among the population in which the moochers, looters and cultural vandals have become increasingly more oppressive to a minority whose frustration and feelings of impotence are escalating rapidly, secession is not an unreasonable consideration where that minority has become a majority and no longer wishes to be subjected to the oppressive whims of the ignorant majority or the oppressive minority.

"Beside the advantage of being armed, which Americans possess over the people of almost every other nation, the existence of subordinate governments, to which the people are attached and militia officers are appointed, forms a barrier against the enterprises of ambition, more insurmountable than any which a simple government of any form can admit of." James Madison

One can hope that a peaceful and equitable solution to the problem of liberty may be found. That the current power will see the wisdom of recognizing the rights and liberties of the people and relinquish their illegitimately usurped authorities. If government is left to its own devices, that is not going to happen. A government that fears nothing will do anything. The only question is how much resistance will be required to force the government to back down from its assault on freedom. There is no question that those in power, when that power is long established in the hands of individuals who are largely unaccountable, accustomed to wielding that power in immoral ways and consumed with the belief in their own entitlement to rule, will go to *any* lengths to maintain that power. Are those who love liberty willing to go to any lengths to assert their rights? If the state is more than willing to plunder, imprison and kill threats to its power, are the defenders of liberty prepared to oppose such tactics with equal vehemence? The answer to that question will determine the fate of freedom individually, nationally and worldwide.

The Morality of Conflict

There will be those who decry such actions, labeling them immoral, unpatriotic and terroristic. For what is terrorism but using intimidation and violence to achieve a political outcome? Yet the government, in order to assure compliance with their legal plunder, encourages fear among the populace. The threats of fines and imprisonment, the harassment and even actual assault and assassination, designed to bring about a political result. They make examples of a minority to ensure the meek compliance of the majority to their political ends. This is terrorism, pure and simple. With such threats and actions, responding in kind against a government that perpetrates such activity is more than justified. Any activities taken against such a government may well be considered *counter-terrorism*.

Even so, such action is offensive to our sensibilities. Our hesitance, while confirming a moral position above our plunderers, is also a hindrance to the defense of our liberty. This is because the statists, who have changed their name many times (Communist-progressive-liberal-socialists) decided that the goal of totalitarian control in America and the West could best be achieved gradually as opposed to the violent revolutions perpetrated in Russia and elsewhere. The incremental imposition of totalitarianism, coupled with a propaganda campaign designed to convince its victims that their bonds were necessary and beneficial, rarely offered a target substantial enough to focus passionate opposition. They changed the way we viewed the role of government, shifting the argument from whether government should be involved in plunder to how the government is going to plunder and for whose benefit.

"There are more instances of the abridgment of the freedom of the people by gradual and silent encroachments of those in power than by violent and sudden usurpations" James Madison

Consider how far we have come along the ten stated communist goals of Marx. We have a "Heavy progressive or graduated tax", with the death tax we are working on the "abolition of the rights of inheritance", the Fed, Fannie and Freddie, SBA and Dodd-Frank have accomplished a "Centralization of credit in the hands of the state, by means of a national bank with state capital and an exclusive monopoly", property taxes and aforementioned court decisions have achieved the

"Abolition of property in land and application of all rents of land to public purposes." We are the only nation to tax people living and working outside our national borders and are considering a tax in emigration resulting in the "Centralization of the property of emigrants and rebels." Through licensing, fees, executive order and a complaint media the "Centralization of the means of communication and transport in the hands of the state" is available. With the bailouts and "investments" the government makes in various industries we are rapidly moving toward "Extension of factories and instruments of production owned by the state." Labor laws, the political clout of unions, particularly government unions, the war on the wealthy and President Obama's call for a civil defense force equal to the military are establishing "Equal liability of all labor. Establishment of industrial armies." The adoption of Agenda 21, the EPA's war on small business and farmers and the radical environmental agenda have laid the groundwork for a "Combination of agriculture with manufacturing industries, gradual abolition of the distinction between town and country but a more equitable distribution of the population over the country." And finally, to ensure a steady stream of compliant automatons who never consider questioning the role of government to regulate every aspect of their lives but look to it as their savior in all things we have established "Free education for all children in public schools."

"You cannot bring about prosperity by discouraging thrift. You cannot strengthen the weak by weakening the strong. You cannot help the wage earner by pulling down the wage payer. You cannot further the brotherhood of man by encouraging class hatred. You cannot keep out of trouble by spending more than you earn. You cannot build character and courage by taking away a man's initiative and independence. You cannot help men permanently by doing what they could and should do for themselves." Abraham Lincoln

We have, or are in the process of, implementing Marx's communist agenda and not a shot has been fired, little opposition has manifested itself. Communism, the elimination of all individual rights for the benefit of the collective, is the very opposite of the personal liberty envisioned by our revolutionary forefathers. If someone one hundred years ago had attempted to inflict this on us all at once, we would have taken up arms in our defense, and rightly so. Had the Soviet Union invaded the United States and attempted to impose such a system, we would have all taken our guns off the mantle and shot every one of the "commie bastards." Yet because it is being compelled from the "inside" over time with lawyers and bureaucrats we meekly submit, occasionally wondering where our freedom has gone while we enjoy a blissfully ignorant ride to the absolute tyranny of a modern totalitarian state. Is there any substantial difference? Does it matter whether your rights are violated by an invading army or an internal police force? Whether it happens over time or all at once? Of course not, a violation of rights is a violation of rights, it is never justified, it is never right. Am I any less justified in defending my life against a murderer from across the street than I am against some jihadist from a foreign country? Of course not. One is no less justified in using *any* means necessary to defend oneself against the "commie bastards" from across the ocean as one is the "commie bastards" in our midst. Our government has no more moral, legal or logical authority to destroy our rights to life, liberty and property than does an invading communist army.

Once we realize that we have been bound through either laziness, ignorance or fear, do we not have every right to rise up in even violent protest against the assault on our lives, liberty and property that our ancestors would have if they had faced it all at once? We now have politicians who are avowed socialists and communists and the vast majority of whom accept and promote most of the communist ideology, accepting the government's role in coercion and plunder. Do we not have the right our founder's exercised, a right enshrined in our founding document? "But when a long train of abuses and usurpations, pursuing invariably the same Object evinces a design to reduce them under absolute Despotism, *it is their right, it is their duty,* to throw off such Government, and to provide new Guards for their future security." As an individual I have the right, indeed the duty as a sovereign human being, to protect myself from any individual or corporate entity that would seek to reduce my humanity by assaulting my rights to life, liberty or property.

"What country can preserve its liberties if its rulers are not warned from time to time that their people preserve the spirit of resistance? Let them take arms." Thomas Jefferson

Conclusion

One can choose to live under an immoral system in varying degrees of comfort, living as a moocher or looter. Millions did in the Soviet Union and billions still live under oppressive regimes today. You can keep your head down, do what you're told, accept your lot and live a life of mundane servitude, raising your children to do the same, every generation sliding deeper into totalitarian slavery. In the socialist welfare states of the West, you can live greedily at the expense of your neighbor, dependent on government loot and according to government regulation for as long as it lasts. Neither system requires anything of you but meek submission and if the state has not yet degenerated into the random, or systemic, brutality characteristic of many around the world, you may live a long, dreary life as a scavenger or beast of burden, one of billions in generations past, present and future who failed to become truly human, exercising the full potential of their faculties as free men, for a mere lack of courage and determination.

In America, the vast majority of our brethren are

shuffling forward, senses dulled with the opiates of state supplied goods, pushing onward toward the cliff to commit suicide on a national scale, proclaiming enthusiastically or with muted resignation that we have freely chosen the instruments of our death and are therefore bound to suffer destruction without resistance or complaint. A nation founded on individual liberty and rights has become a corporate herd of slaves who vote for their chains and regard those who hold freedom in esteem with the highest contempt, desiring to drag them along to endure the fate of all totalitarian regimes.

Are you going to allow yourself to be dragged along with the subservient mob, plunging over the cliff with the lemmings? What is your point of surrender? When is the cost of living as a free man or woman, as a human being, too high? The brave and courageous men pledged their lives, fortunes and sacred honor to fight an empire that merely wanted to impose a few taxes because they saw the necessity of meeting and fighting any threat to liberty as worth the sacrifice. We are subjected to much worse while most believe we are still the "land of the free and the home of the brave." We have compromised with evil, drinking the poison of statism thinking we could combine the morality of liberty with the depravity of plunder and dependence. There can be no compromise between the two, it is either one or the other. We deceive ourselves if we think otherwise.

The choice lies with us. It is the ability to

choose our destiny that makes us unique creatures in God's creation. When we are confronted with the choice we face today, and every day, whether we will live as free men and women or not, whether we will live morally or at the expense of others, we will weigh the consequences of each and make our decision. Are the sacrifices for liberty and morality right, are they worth fighting for, are they worth dying for? You must answer that question as must I. The future of our children and grandchildren, that of the noble experiment for which the founders gave all and indeed, the fate of freedom in the world will hinge upon the decision you and I make.

"The cause of America is in a great measure the cause of all mankind." Thomas Paine

I have, at times, referenced specific books, web sites or organizations in this book. Such mentions do not expressly or implicitly imply an endorsement by by me of their work nor they of mine. I have personally found their information helpful and accurate and believe it will be beneficial to other patriots. Here are some other sources of information you may find helpful.

Reading List-by no means exhaustive

On Liberty Frederic Bastiat

The Road to Serfdom F.A Hayek

Capitalism; The Unknown Ideal Ayn Rand

The Art of War

Cracking the Code; The fascinating Truth About Taxation in America Peter Eric Hendrickson

Citizen Soldier; A Manual of Community Based Defense Robert Bradley

Leave Me Alone; A Patriot's Plan for Restoring Pride and Prosperity in America Michael Calpino

Trickle up Poverty/Trickle Down Tyranny Michael Savage

www.ingramcontent.com/pod-product-compliance
Lightning Source LLC
Chambersburg PA
CBHW072229170526
45158CB00002BA/824